URGENT!

SAVE OUR OCEAN TO SURVIVE CLIMATE CHANGE

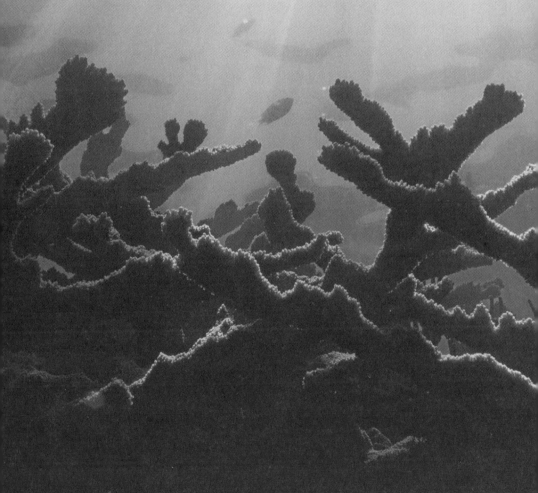

URGENT!

SAVE OUR OCEAN TO SURVIVE CLIMATE CHANGE

Captain Paul Watson

Groundswell Books
Summertown, Tennessee

Library of Congress Cataloging-in-Publication Data available upon request.

We chose to print this title on sustainably harvested paper stock certified by the Forest Stewardship Council, an independent auditor of responsible forestry practices. For more information, visit us.fsc.org.

Photos courtesy of Paul Watson: pp. 7, 50, 86
Photos courtesy of Sea Shepherd: pp. vi, 3, 4, 13, 38, 48, 56, 75, 89
Stock photography: 123 RF
Cover and interior design: John Wincek, aerocraftart.com

Printed in the United States of America

Groundswell Books
an imprint of BPC
PO Box 99
Summertown, TN 38483
888-260-8458
bookpubco.com

ISBN: 978-1-57067-403-7

26 25 24 23 22 21   1 2 3 4 5 6 7 8 9

CONTENTS

From the Sea

My name is Paul Franklin Watson. I was born on December 2, 1950, and grew up in a Canadian fishing village along the Atlantic Coast on Passamaquoddy Bay. I have spent most of my life upon salt water, from the Arctic to the Antarctic and the tropical and temperate latitudes in between. I've been on the decks of Scandinavian merchant ships crisscrossing the Indian and Pacific Oceans, Canadian Coast Guard weather ships, lighthouse supply vessels, and search-and-rescue vessels on the coast of British Columbia.

I have never been on a fishing vessel. My childhood memories of the destruction and slaughter perpetrated by the fishing industry soured me from ever serving on decks soaked in blood, fish guts, and misery.

Most proudly, I have sailed for marine conservation, first as an officer on Greenpeace ships beginning in 1971, and since 1978, as captain on the ships of Sea Shepherd Conservation Society, an organization (now a global movement)

that I founded in 1977. I have sailed to oppose nuclear weapons testing and to save whales, dolphins, seals, sea turtles, and sharks. I have sailed to stop illegal fishing vessels, to rescue animals from oil spills, and to remove plastic debris from the ocean. I have sailed to increase global awareness of the damage humanity has inflicted on aquatic life and diversity, and, even more importantly, to educate people about the imperative need to stop our ecological insanity before we reach the tipping point of no return.

In June 1975, I had an experience that dramatically and positively changed the course of my life. I came face to face with an alien intelligence that would shape and redefine my future.

It happened about one hundred kilometers off the coast of Northern California. I was the first officer on the vessel *Phyllis Cormack*, also called *Greenpeace V*. There were thirteen of us on that small vessel, and our absurdly Quixotic mission was to stop the Soviet whaling fleet. We had been studying the tactics of Mahatma Gandhi, and our basic plan was to simply block the harpoons by placing our bodies between the whales and the whalers, which is exactly what we did.

A Soviet killer boat was in full pursuit of a pod of eight sperm whales. We launched our small inflatable boats and set off on a course to intercept the chase. Robert Hunter (one of the founders of Greenpeace) and I were in the first boat, and I quickly raced to a spot between the hunter and the hunted. Behind us was this huge, rust-blotched steel ship bearing down on us at 20 knots. Looking up, I could see a large man with a dirty white shirt, cigarette clenched between his teeth, crouching behind a baby-blue harpoon cannon with the tip of the explosive projectile aimed straight at us. Looking ahead, we could see that there were eight magnificent sperm whales desperately fleeing for their lives. We could also see their misty blows tinted with the colors of the rainbow. We were so close that we could feel the spray and smell the fear in their every struggling breath.

I reached over, grabbed Robert's hand, and shouted, "We're doing it!"

And, for a few minutes, we were doing what we came to do: we were blocking the harpooner, confident that he would not risk killing us in order to kill a whale.

But then a big man came running down the catwalk from the wheelhouse. It was the Soviet captain. He grabbed the harpooner and shouted into his ear. Then he looked down at us, smiled, and slashed his finger across his throat. The realization hit us that the tactics of Gandhi were not going to work for us that day.

A few moments later, the harpoon fired, and this meter-and-a-half-long projectile whistled over our heads and slammed into the backside of a female in the pod. A shower of blood erupted from

her body as the harpoon exploded. Six of the whales swam on, but the largest whale, the bull, rose up, slapped the water's surface with a thunderous clap, and dove beneath us, only to rise up behind us to challenge the monster that just took the life of one of his family.

They were ready for him. The harpooner had quickly rammed an unattached harpoon into the barrel and set another charge. He swung the cannon around and down and fired, catching the charging cachalot with a point-blank shot to the head. A startling scream of pain echoed across the water as the mortally wounded whale fell back into the sea, roiling in agony upon the surface while a scarlet blanket of hot blood spread out around him.

We were transfixed by the horror of what we were seeing when, suddenly, the whale turned. I caught his eye and he dove once again, leaving a trail of frothy pinkish blood and bubbles as he advanced rapidly toward us. When he got closer, his head rose up from the surface at an angle as he was preparing to fall upon us. That is when my life changed in an instant. There before me, within a meter, was his eye, an orb the size of my fist. It was so close I could see my own reflection in it, and I saw what he was seeing. At that moment, what I sensed and what I felt stunned me. I perceived that he understood what we had tried to do because he made a visible effort to fall backward. His head began to sink into the dark water. I saw his eye disappear below the surface, and then he vanished.

He could have killed us, and the only reason that I am able to write this book is because he chose to spare us. But there was something else, something more that I felt. It was pity. Not for him or for his family but for us. How could we kill so mercilessly and with such brutal cruelty?

The sun was setting, and the lights on the Soviet fleet of four ships and the factory ship, the *Dalniy Vostok*, were flickering on in a circle around me. They were hauling in the bleeding corpses of the two whales, and an incredible sadness crept over me.

Why? Why were they killing these whales? It was not for meat; sperm whale meat is inedible. They were slaughtered for oil, a very high-grade, heat-resistant oil for lubricating machinery. One of the uses for this oil by the Soviet Union was in the manufacturing of intercontinental ballistic missiles.

Their true intent hit me like a slap in the face. Here they were, thoughtlessly killing these beautiful, socially complex, highly intelligent, self-aware, sentient beings for no reason other than to make a weapon designed for the mass incineration and extermination of other human beings. This sudden realization was also a revelation: We're insane. We are grossly and perversely insane.

It was that traumatic awakening to the savage ecological insanity of humanity that dramatically changed the course of my life. From that day on, I have dedicated my life to serving and saving the whales and the other citizens of the sea. I was done with humanity. I rejected the anthropocentric conceit that has guided human evolution since the beginning of agriculture.

Instead, I began to embrace biocentrism, which is the understanding that we all are part of everything, not the master of other species and certainly not the overlords of this planet that we think we are. Every bee, every tree, every worm, every tiny zooplankton and phytoplankton is working hard to maintain the ecological integrity of this planet, while we humans do little but entertain ourselves at the expense of all other species. The dictatorship of our species has been viciously destructive, and it is leading humanity toward a place where it makes no sense to go—our own extinction.

Pandora's Box

When I sat down to begin writing this book, the following was reported in the media: Antarctica logs the hottest temperature on record at 20.75 degrees Celsius (69.35 degrees F). The runaway train has picked up speed. When my son, Tiger, turns seventy in 2086, what will his world be like? I can't even begin to imagine the world he will inherit.

Tiger was conceived in Paris and born September 2016 in New Hampshire in the United States. Today I watched him playing in the snow, laughing and happy, and my heart skipped a beat. But then I suddenly realized that the innocence and joy I was observing may not be something he'll be able to experience when he reaches my age.

I have lived a life of relative material plenty and freedom that future generations may never have because my generation, the generations before me, and the generation of today have made decisions that will rob our children, our grandchildren, and our great-grandchildren of the essential treasures of life,

7

such as joy, happiness, and security. To paraphrase Greta Thunberg, our future has been stolen.

Tiger is facing a future of uncertainty, a future of chaos and sacrifice unlike any generation before him and certainly unlike my childhood. Will he have the opportunity for an academic education or will he be forced to be educated about how to survive? What will he think of his mother and me? How did we let this happen and why? Will his generation despise those that came before them? I wouldn't blame them if they do, but I need my son to know that I cared and that I devoted my life to trying to prevent the world that he may inherit.

As I look at him playing joyfully in the snow, a darker thought nags me. Will my boy have a happy life or am I looking at a future survivalist? Were we selfish to bring him into this world with an uncertain destiny? I can't shield him from the reality of climate change, but can I teach him to survive and be a leader?

I don't have a choice. There can be no hiding from the grim reality. As I write this page, 100,000 square kilometers of Australia have burned in the last week. The scale of that devastation is hard to fathom. These fires are worse than the Amazon, Siberia, and California fires combined:

Amazon fires: 11,587 square kilometers
Siberia fires: 18,507 square kilometers
California fires: 1,480 square kilometers
Total: 31,574 square kilometers

Brittany is 17,000 square kilometers. The fires would equal one-fifth of all the land of France. Or let's compare it to that recent famous fire in Paris, the cathedral of Notre Dame du Paris. Paris is about 105 square miles, which means the Australian fires are equal to 952 cities the size of Paris burning at the same time. Or perhaps this visualization might be more impressive: Notre Dame du Paris is 128 meters long and 157 meters wide. Therefore, the fires represent twenty-one million Notre Dame du Paris cathedrals engulfed in flames.

Within weeks of the firestorms, Australia was hit with flooding, dust storms, and hailstorms. These were destructive hailstorms in the middle of summer in Canberra and New South Wales! For all the climate-change deniers, try denying *that*. Or don't, and watch it all happen over and over and over again, and not just in Australia.

WELCOME TO THERMAGEDDON

The late great Robert Hunter, in his book *Thermageddon*, predicted in 2002 that there would be escalating environmental consequences by 2030. He was overly optimistic. We are seeing this escalation a full decade before the one he predicted.

What is happening in Australia now is just the beginning. The Pandora's box of climate change has been opened, and the repercussions of our ecological sins are rushing out to devour us. Can we keep the lid on the box long enough to learn how to survive the consequences that are spilling out around the edges and into our ecosystems, dramatically changing the mechanisms of our life-support systems at an ever-escalating pace?

I am not writing this book to address the question of stopping climate change. That ship left the harbor years ago and will not be returning. We had our chances and we let them slip away. The reality is that we can't stop it. We may be able to mitigate the consequences, but the juggernaut has been released; it's on the run, and humankind is very slowly becoming aware of the forces that have been let loose from the dark and unpredictable Pandora's box that humanity fabricated.

I am writing this book not so much for the purpose of helping others understand the problem but rather for the purpose of our collective survival. However, the first step in addressing a problem is acknowledging that the problem exists and comprehending the nature of the threat.

There is only one effective way for this threat to be challenged, and that is on a political level. The scientists have spoken, but they have been ignored. The media, for the most part, have been bought off by the corporations that own and control global messaging and that have spent billions to downplay and dismiss the science of climate change. In order for us to effectively address climate change, we must implement policies that involve material sacrifice, which major corporations and world leaders simply refuse to undertake.

The immediate solution requires the cessation or dramatic reduction of the consumption of fossil fuels. It requires an end to the mass slaughter of seventy-two billion domestic animals every year by the meat industry. It requires broad curtailment of industrialized fishing to stop the collapse of oceanic ecosystems. It requires the dismantling of the global military industrial complex. It requires wide-ranging restrictions on the use of pesticides, fungicides, herbicides, and industrial fertilizers. And, above all, it requires a significant reduction of both human populations and the consumption of natural resources by every human being on the planet.

These are not plans that any politician today can practically promote, and that is why every single climate change conference since they first began in 1979 has failed to provide workable solutions.

When I was in high school, I told my father that if he did not quit smoking he would die of lung cancer. He replied, "I'll cross that bridge when I come to it." Twenty years later, he did quit smoking, but twenty years after that he died . . . of lung cancer. I remember how mystified he was that he was actually dying of cancer. He continued to be in denial that smoking was the cause, since, after all, he had quit.

And that is where we are today. Politicians and CEOs of corporations have seen the warnings but have chosen to ignore and deny them. Even with forests burning, sea levels rising, storms increasing and intensifying, and glaciers retreating, they insist that the problem is not of their making and that they can't do anything to stop it. A few world leaders have actually suggested that climate change may be a *good* thing because it gives us increased growing seasons and warmer weather, even though the reality is far different.

What will stop it will be actual destructive consequences. In fact, in March 2020 we began to experience what these consequences will be. One of the deadly manifestations of climate change is the emergence of new viruses. Some of these are released from centuries of hibernation in the now-melting permafrost. Others are created by the meat industry, particularly by "wet markets" where exotic wildlife are slaughtered, causing viruses from different species to jump onto human hosts. As other species are diminished or driven to extinction, the viruses long associated with these different species are forced to find new hosts, and the very large, densely packed human populations are the most convenient hosts for these pathogens.

Addiction

I n Alcoholics Anonymous, the first rule is to accept the fact that you're an addict. "Hello. My name is Paul Watson, and I'm addicted to this black substance called oil." Crude oil, to be exact. And it is, in every sense of the word, a drug.

Like most people reading this book, I "consume" oil when I drive, when I fly in airplanes, when I eat food produced with fertilizers, and when I use plastic, along with numerous other instances. I am a much bigger oil addict than many other people. I command anti-poaching ships that, although laudable for hunting poachers, consume thousands of barrels of oil every year. I justify our addiction by shutting down illegal fishing vessels, which overall means that we prevent more carbon from being released into the atmosphere than we consume. We compare the amount of fuel we consume to the amount of fuel we prevent from being consumed by the vessels we arrest and seize. We also justify our consumption with the knowledge that we cannot do our job without using ships.

13

Unfortunately, this is the same justification that pertains to most people. Oil is the substance that drives the worldwide economy. This means that, despite the efforts we make and the successes we have had in our conservation activities, we still are like most everyone else: ecological criminals.

What can we do about it? We could shut down operations and allow the poachers free rein to continue their destruction of oceanic ecosystems. Sea Shepherd has one sailing vessel, but it is pointless to replace all our engine-driven vessels with sails because the poachers would simply outrun us. We can't abandon the lives of the species we defend, but at the same time, there is no escaping the fact that we are hypocrites in a world populated and dominated by hypocrites.

In other words, we are all guilty. If you have a birth certificate, that is sufficient evidence of guilt. From birth to death we consume oil, from disposable diapers to coffins and cremation. Even if we want to change our lifestyles—by never flying, by boycotting products transported by trucks, by not buying anything that requires the operation of machinery or the use of fertilizers—can we? Can eight billion people survive without the consumption of oil, coal, and gas?

Sadly, and truthfully, the realistic answer to this question is no. So, having admitted our addiction, we need to confront the scope of it. How extensive and how destructive is this addiction, and can we ever remove this colossal greasy monkey from our backs?

The global consumption of oil is around 93,500,000 barrels each day. The United States consumes 19,530,000 barrels per day; followed by China, with 11,120,000; and Japan, at 4,120,000. France ranks thirteenth, consuming on average 1,691,000 barrels per day. This is the substance our entire civilization is addicted to for driving, flying, cruising, and heating, as well as for generating power, making fertilizers, providing entertainment, and producing plastics.

Humans have taken on the behavior of mosquitoes as we suck the planet dry of fossil fuels. And there's no doubt about it, we *will* suck it dry. The "law of finite resources" is quite firm concerning the limited supplies of oil, gas, and coal. The fossil fuel industry *will* collapse. The only question is when.

Imagine a world without fossil fuels. It won't be pleasant. It will be a return to sailing ships and horses. My most optimistic vision of the year 2120 is that it will be somewhat akin to the year 1820. My least optimistic vision is the world depicted in the film *Mad Max* but without the cars. My most pessimistic vision is a sterile world, like the end days of the great Permian extinction.

Before any of these scenarios occur, however, there will be a dramatic decline of human populations triggered by our own over-population and overconsumption of resources and the emergence of

novel viruses. This will be coupled with the escalating reduction of other species, leading to an accelerated depletion of resources caused by infrastructure collapse, crop failures, epidemics, and resource-based wars. The outlook does not look good.

It is not my intention to ease minds with false promises and false hopes. The future is not looking like a pretty picture. We have to face the reality that the challenges ahead are formidable and the prospects for survival are daunting.

I only need to look at the coral reefs to see how serious a problem climate change is. Coral is not just bleaching; it is currently dissolving and dying at an alarming rate around the world. Bleaching occurs when coral is stressed by warmer water and increased acidification, causing the coral to lose its symbiotic algae. It is the algae that gives coral its color. Unlike humans, however, some corals are adapting to climate change by moving into deeper subtropical and cooler waters. Tropical reefs have declined by 85 percent, while there has simultaneously been a 78 percent increase in coral propagation outside of tropical waters.

This does not bode well for tropical coral reefs. By 2100, the outlook is for a world devoid of tropical coral reef systems. Some corals may adapt and survive, but tropical coral reef ecosystems may not, and that will be a death sentence for thousands of tropical species.

One group, the Scleractinia, or stony corals, were able to survive the Cretaceous–Tertiary extinction by going into deeper waters, and they appear to be preparing to do the same again for the current Anthropocene event. Unlike coral, humans are not showing any real signs of adapting. Does humanity have the capacity to make the sacrifices required to live in a world without the use of fossil fuels? Fossil fuel resources will be exhausted within the next century. Will people look up from their amusements and distractions before it is far too late?

DRIVING TOWARD EXTINCTION

It is estimated that there are roughly 1.3 billion motor vehicles in operation on the planet. On top of that, there are two million snowmobiles in North America and some twelve million motorcycles in operation, not to mention billions of lawn mowers, snowblowers, leaf blowers, chainsaws, and millions of other fossil-fueled machines. Every second of every minute of every hour of every day, tens of thousands of liters of liquid petrol and diesel get transformed into carbon emissions. It is a constant and never-ending cycle.

Since the dawn of the Industrial Revolution, the conversion of stored carbon into the atmosphere has been continuous and increasing more and more every year. When this began, carbon dioxide in the atmosphere was about 280 ppm (parts per million). It is now surpassing 400 ppm—a 39 percent increase. This is the highest concentration in two million years. Methane concentrations have risen from 715 ppm in 1750 to close to 2,000 ppm today. The regular daily shedding of plastic particles from billions of tires is a major source of microplastics in aquatic ecosystems. In every sense, we are driving toward our own extinction.

FLYING TOWARD EXTINCTION

Travel and the movement of goods by air is an industry just over a century old. Every day, at any given moment, there are between thirteen and sixteen thousand planes in the sky. Each day, approximately 7,700,000 people fly. This works out to more than an average of 3.2 million people in the air every hour of every day. More than three billion passenger seats are sold each year. Every moment of the day there is a moving mega-city in the air. As I write this sentence, I am on a United Airlines flight between Los Angeles and Boston.

Add to this the number of military aircraft in the sky. The United States has the largest number of military aircraft at 13,398. Russia is second at 4,078. China is third at 3,187. India is fourth at 2,082. South Korea ranks fifth with 1,614. Japan ranks sixth with 1,572. Pakistan ranks seventh with 1,342. France ranks eighth with 1,248. When we also include cargo aircraft, small recreational aircraft, and helicopters, it's easy to see that the amount of fossil fuels consumed by aircraft alone is immense. The estimate for fuel consumption by commercial airlines is ninety-eight billion gallons annually.

CRUISING TOWARD EXTINCTION

For thousands of years, ocean travel was undertaken by sail. Less than two hundred years ago, sail was replaced by steam, and around one hundred years later, steam was replaced by huge engines burning diesel or the heavier and dirtier Bunker C oil. This year, about twenty-nine million people will purchase passages on cruise ships. The average consumption of fuel by a cruise ship is about three hundred tons per day. For example, the cruise ship *Freedom of the Sea* (1,112 feet) burns twenty-eight thousand gallons per hour.

The top 314 passenger cruise ships total 537,000 berths, with a market of over twenty-six million passengers each year. If the average consumption is 300 hundred tons of fuel per day, that would be a daily consumption rate of 94,200 tons of fuel each day just for the top 314 vessels, with over 34 million tons in total.

There are also over 350,000 smaller cruise ships operating on seas, lakes, and rivers. This means that every person who takes a cruise is contributing to one of the most energy-consuming for-pleasure-only industries. Cruise ships do not move goods of necessity. They produce excessive sewage and organic and plastic waste, in addition to their excessive production of carbon emissions. Cruise ship passage did receive a major blow in March 2020 with the emergence of the COVID-19 virus. Large cruise ships have emerged as very dangerous places to be during a pandemic, as they become, in effect, large floating petri dishes.

EATING OUR WAY TOWARD EXTINCTION

We slaughter sixty-five billion domestic animals every year and extract billions of fish from the sea. Raising animals for meat is the primary cause for dead zones in the ocean, the primary cause for groundwater pollution, and a greater source of greenhouse gas emissions than the entire transportation industry. About 40 percent of the fish taken are fed directly to domestic animals, such as chickens, pigs, and farmed salmon. The bycatch waste from the fisheries is measured in the millions of tons. Eight billion flesh-eating hominid primates represent a planet completely out of balance with nature. We are literally eating our way toward our own extinction.

WHAT DOES IT ALL MEAN?

'm not going to list all the facts and statistics; such data is available for anyone who wishes to research it. I just want to briefly illustrate the shocking magnitude of our resource consumption. The message here is that the problem is incredibly immense and complex and the solution is seemingly impossible. However, I have always held the opinion that the answer to an impossible problem is to use our passion and imagination to find the possible solution.

In 1972, the very idea that Nelson Mandela would someday be president of South Africa was unthinkable and seemingly impossible, but that impossibility became possible. Unfortunately, we have never had an impossible problem like climate change, a global predicament impacting the entire world, during which humanity has not only failed to act but continues to fail to act.

I am not a pessimist; I am a realist. The writing is very much on the wall in bold flashing letters. Our entire species is threatened, along with hundreds of thousands of other species that will sink into oblivion with us unless we address the threats boldly, courageously, and passionately. To do that we need to see the entire picture and understand the causes and then work to implement the solutions. If we fail to do this, how can we survive?

This Has All Happened Before

There are some people who don't deny the reality of climate change but insist that the cause isn't humanity. Often the rationale for their viewpoint is that since climate change has occurred before it must be natural. In one sense, they are right. This has all happened before, and, yes, humanity was not responsible. However, although the problem (greenhouse gas emissions) is the same, the previous triggers for it were different. This time around, humanity is indeed the trigger.

Sadly, whenever dramatic climate change has occurred, it did not bode well for the majority of species existing at the time. About 252 million years ago, our planet experienced the greatest ecological catastrophe in natural history. It was called the Permian–Triassic extinction event, also known as the Great Dying. It's estimated that 96 percent of all marine species and 70 percent of all terrestrial vertebrate species became extinct. It was also the largest extinction event for insects, with 57 percent of biological families obliterated.

The primary cause for this mass extinction was climate change brought on by one or more possible impacts from an asteroid, along with intensified volcanic activity in the Siberian region, massive prolonged burning of coal deposits, and methane hydrate gasification. In short, there was an overproduction of carbon dioxide and methane. Increased CO_2 production led to dangerous levels of acidification. The asteroid impact or the volcanic activity or both could have been the trigger. Whatever the cause, there was runaway climate change, and it took Earth about eighteen million years to recover.

All living things manufacture the chemicals and gases that maintain life on this planet. Plants produce oxygen; animals produce carbon dioxide. These two gases need to be stabilized by each other, and when they are, the system works beautifully. That is, it works beautifully until something interferes, such as volcanoes, asteroids, massive releases of methane from the sea or from permafrost, or willful emissions caused by a single species, such as humans.

Another possible contributing factor to the Great Dying was the emergence of anaerobic methanogenic archaea, an evolution of microbes that could metabolize acetate into methane. A rapid escalation in global populations of these microbes could have produced massive amounts of methane and carbon dioxide.

The Permian–Triassic extinction did not happen overnight. It actually took seventy thousand years for the biosphere to fully collapse the way it did. The good news is that Earth recovered and was more vibrant, more diverse, and even more prolific than before the Great Dying.

The Permian–Triassic was actually the third mass extinction event. The first was the Ordovician–Silurian extinction event 439 million years ago that wiped out about 87 percent of all life on the planet. Again, the cause was climate change, but the stimulus was different. There was a dangerous decline in carbon dioxide because of prolific vegetation, and that was coupled with a severe lowering of sea levels induced by plate tectonics.

The second mass extinction was the Late Devonian event, which took place 364 million years ago and incurred the loss of 75 percent of all species. The upside is that if it weren't for the Late Devonian aftermath, we humans would probably not exist today. Life in the sea was greatly diminished by this event, and about ten million years after it occurred, the ichthyostegalians—an order of now-extinct amphibians representing the earliest land-living vertebrates—crawled onto solid ground. It is from these amphibians that all terrestrial animals evolved.

The third mass extinction event, the Permian–Triassic, was followed by the Triassic–Jurassic, which took place between 199 million and 214 million years ago. Once more, the cause was possible impact, intense volcanism, and climate change. This period was followed by the rise of the dinosaurs.

The fifth extinction was the Cretaceous–Paleogene extinction event that brought an end to the age of dinosaurs and ushered in the world we have today. The event wiped out 76 percent of life on the planet. The primary cause is believed to be a massive asteroid impact near the Yucatan Peninsula in Mexico. Again, there is an upside. Without this mass extinction event, humanity would most likely not exist today, although it is quite possible that an intelligent saurian species could have evolved and been capable of building a technological society.

So where are we now? We are at the beginning of the Holocene extinction era, also called the Anthropocene. This time it is not an asteroid or intense volcanism that is responsible. For the first time in the history of the planet, we are facing an extinction event brought on by the behavior and actions of a single species: *Homo sapiens*. Our activities have increased species extinction at an alarming rate, and our willful release of greenhouse gases, such as carbon dioxide, is triggering massive methane releases from permafrost and the sea.

Let's take a look at just what this planet is to us. We know Earth came into being more than four billion years ago, and for most of that time, there was no life on this relatively tiny bit of rock. But life did begin, at first clinging to the rocks in little patches of microbial colonies that set in motion the process that we call evolution. Life constructed a support system for itself on Earth. This life-support system is what keeps us alive today. Our incredibly diverse ecosystems within the global biosphere produce the air we breathe via the plants, and the carbon dioxide that we animals produce sustains the plants, thereby allowing for respiration. This life-support system feeds us, cleans and recycles waste, regulates climates, regulates temperatures, and moves nutrients through the winds and the tides and the lakes and the bodies of untold billions of organisms. What started as barren rock began to retain water, forming what today is a celestial body that should really be called the water planet or planet Ocean.

Climate change is impacting seawater through the escalated dissolving of carbon, which causes increased acidification. This is resulting in coral bleaching and the weakening of exoskeletons in invertebrate species. Excessive CO_2 emissions are increasing the acidity of precipitation, resulting in tree-destroying acid rain.

Climate change is impacting ice by converting the massive amounts of solid water into liquid, leading to rising sea levels. Glacial activity is also an important source for delivering iron into aquatic ecosystems, which provide a major source of nutrients for phytoplankton.

Climate change is affecting the water in the atmosphere with temperature disparities that intensify storms and cause geographical fluctuations that result in periods of drought and precipitation. Excess precipitation brings flooding, and prolonged drought brings about both desertification and intense bush and forest fires.

The processes involved in resolving these conditions accelerate climate change in an ever-increasing feedback loop. Melting ice exposes more open water in the Arctic. Without the ice to reflect the heat, the water absorbs the heat and becomes even warmer. Bush and forest fires spew carbon dioxide into the atmosphere. The Australian bush fires of 2019–2020 emitted over 250 million tons of CO_2. These emissions alone are almost equal to the annual emissions (271 million tons) of our planet's approximately 150 million active volcanoes. The estimated carbon dioxide emissions caused by human activity are approximately 40 billion metric tons per year and about sixty times that of all the current volcanic emissions. Since the beginning of the Industrial Revolution, human activity has produced about two thousand billion tons of carbon dioxide.

Let's revisit the Permian–Triassic extinction. Scientists estimated that between two and three thousand billion tons of carbon were released in the form of carbon dioxide and methane. The maximum concentration of CO_2 during the Permian–Triassic extinction was 3,550 ppm (parts per million). The ppm during the early Permian–Triassic extinction was about the same as today, and the average over eighteen thousand years was about 900 ppm.

The amount of carbon dioxide in the atmosphere prior to the Industrial Revolution was 280 ppm. Today it is 409 ppm, the highest level in four hundred thousand years. It rises every year at a rate faster than the early days of the Permian–Triassic event. In short, this rising rate is just under half the average during the Permian–Triassic extinction, and that is very concerning. The reality is that the human species cannot survive the level of a Permian–Triassic climate-change event or even an event with one-tenth the CO_2 levels of the Permian–Triassic.

We Are the Ocean

would like to introduce you to an alternative way of looking at this planet that we live on. We call it planet Earth, but in reality it is planet Ocean. What makes life possible on this planet is one very important element: water. This is the water planet. We have been taught that the ocean is the sea. However, the ocean is much more than that.

This is a planet of water in continuous circulation through many phases, intimately linked at every stage. It is the water in the sea, the lakes, the rivers, and the streams. It is the water flowing underground and deep, deep down inside the planet, locked in rock. It is the water in the atmosphere or encased in ice. And it is the water moving through each and every living cell of every plant and animal on the planet.

It is the blood of the living planet—sometimes a liquid, sometimes a solid, sometimes a gas—constantly moving from one stage to the next and to the next and back again. It is an element with unique properties so amazing that it does not conform even to the laws that govern its existence. It's lighter as a solid than as a liquid, for example, and if not for this factor, the planet would be completely encased in ice from the seafloor to the outer edge of where the atmosphere is today. If it were heavier as a solid, it would sink and sink until the entire sea was solid.

Water has a memory and sometimes seems to be alive. Why else would a still pond not be frozen at temperatures below freezing, yet when a pebble is tossed into it, the pond begins to freeze immediately, as if it were just woken up and reminded that the temperature demands that it freeze.

Water is life, powered by the sun pumping it from sea to atmosphere and into and through our every living cell. Water is the life that flows through our bodies, flushing out waste and supplying nutrients. The water in my body now was once locked in ice. It once moved underground. It once was in the clouds or in the sea. And the same water was once drunk and pissed out by dinosaurs. Even the gravitational pull of the moon acts on the water in our bodies in the same way it acts upon the water in the sea. Water is the common bond of all living things on this planet, and, collectively, all this water in its many forms and travels is the one ocean.

The ocean is the life-support system for the entire planet. From within the depths of the sea, phytoplankton manufactures oxygen while feeding on nitrogen and iron supplied from the feces of whales and other marine animals. The water in rivers and lakes removes toxins, salts, and waste. Estuaries and wetlands act like the kidneys to remove toxins, and the mineral salts are flushed into the sea. The heat from the sun pumps water into the atmosphere, where it is purified and dropped back onto the surface of the planet, where living things drink or absorb it before flushing it through their systems. It is this complex global circulatory system that provides everything we need for food, sanitation, and the regulation of climate—for life.

Water is life and life is water. Rivers and streams are the arteries, veins, and capillaries of the earth, performing the very same functions that they do in our bodies: remove waste and deliver nutrients to cells. When a river is dammed, it is akin to cutting off the flow in a blood vessel. For example, the great Aswan High Dam on the Nile River starved the lands below of nutrients, building up toxic waters above.

This entire interdependent system is its own life-support system. The book *Gaia* by James Lovelock is a hypothesis proposing that all living organisms interact with their inorganic surroundings to form a synergistic and self-regulating complex system that helps maintain and perpetuate the conditions for life on the planet. In other words, life operates its own life-support system. In this system, not all species are equal. Some species are essential and some species are less so, but all species are connected. The essential foundations of this life-support system are microbes, phytoplankton, insects, plants, worms, and fungi. The so-called "higher" animals are not so essential, and one of them—humans and the domesticated animal and plant slaves we own—are alarmingly destructive.

I like to compare Earth to a spaceship. After all, that is what this planet is—a huge spaceship transporting the cargo of life on a fast and furious trip around the enormous Milky Way galaxy. It's a voyage so long that it takes about 250 million years to make just one circumnavigation. In fact, our planet has only made this trip eighteen times since it was formed from the dust of our closest star.

For a spaceship to function, there needs to be a well-run life-support system that is managed by an experienced and skillful crew. It is this crew that produces the gases in our atmosphere, especially oxygen, nitrogen, and carbon dioxide. It is this crew that sequesters excess gases, particularly carbon and methane. It is this crew that cleans the air, recycles waste, and assists in the circulation of water. It also supplies food, both directly and indirectly through pollination. It is this crew that removes toxins from the soil and keeps the soil moist and productive. The plants serve the animals and the animals serve the plants. The plants feed on the sun and the animals feed on the plants, and, in turn, the animals impart nutrients to the soil.

Some species, especially the ones we call the "higher" animals (mainly the large mammals), are primarily passengers. Some of these passengers contribute a great deal to maintaining the machinery of the life-support system, although they are not as critical as the absolutely essential species that serve as the tireless engineers of the system. There is one passenger species, however, that long ago decided to mutiny from the crew and go its own way, content to spend its days entertaining itself and caring only for its own welfare. That species is *Homo sapiens*.

There are other species, both plant and animal, that we have enslaved for our own selfish purposes. These are the domesticated plants that replace the wild plants that help run the system. These are the animals that we have enslaved to give us meat, eggs, and milk, or to serve the purpose of amusing us, only to be abused, tortured, and slaughtered.

As the number of enslaved animals increases, wild animals are displaced through extermination or the destruction of habitat. The plants that we enslave must be "protected" with lethal chemical fertilizers and genetically modified seeds, along with other chemical poisons, such as herbicides, fungicides, and bactericides.

We are stealing the carrying capacity of ecosystems from other species to increase the number of humans and domestic animals. The law of finite resources dictates that this system will collapse. It simply is unsustainable.

Because of our technological skills, humans have evolved to serve one very important function: We have the ability to protect the entire planet from being struck by a killer asteroid like the one that paid our dinosaur friends a visit sixty million years ago. Although I sometimes wonder if we could even do that, considering our lack of cooperation within our own species. We also have the skills and intelligence, if we so choose to utilize these abilities, to aggressively address climate change, the problem that we are directly responsible for creating. But will we?

Obstacles

E xtraction-industry corporations control every aspect of global society. That's where the money is, and that money controls politics and mainstream media. That control comes from literally owning politicians and media outlets. The issue for environmentalists and climate change activists is not just fabricated and distorted news. Rather, it's the absence of news. It is all the issues that are deliberately, willfully, and strategically ignored.

Since 2011, we have heard very little about the Fukushima Daiichi nuclear disaster, despite the fact that radioactive water is being dumped into the sea and radioactive groundwater is creeping slowly toward Tokyo. We also hear very little about the murders of environmentalists, especially Indigenous activists. Between the year 2000 and 2013, more than one thousand environmentalists were murdered. This number only reflects what is in official reports; the actual numbers are most likely higher. Since 2013, we can add another thousand assassinations. Ominously,

the killings are escalating. Forty percent of the victims have been Indigenous people, such as mining and dam opponent Berta Cáceres of Honduras, who was murdered in 2017. Only a very small fraction of the cases for these killings have been solved. The killers tend to murder with impunity and without much, if any, media coverage or public reaction.

In 2013, I had to offer a reward of $30,000 for information on the killers of Jairo Mora Sandoval, the twenty-six-year-old conservationist who was brutally murdered in Costa Rica while attempting to protect leatherback turtle nests. The killers were apprehended and then released because the evidence was lost by the police. Fortunately, public outrage resulted in a second trial and conviction. The following numbers are shocking, but even more so because the public is mostly unaware of the killings.

ESTIMATED NUMBER OF MURDERS OF ENVIRONMENTAL ACTIVISTS BY YEAR

2013	2014	2015	2016	2017	2018	TOTAL
160	116	185	200	207	164	1,032

Among those who have been murdered were observers on fishing vessels, park rangers, lawyers and lawmakers, union organizers, conservationists, environmentalists, Indigenous leaders, and activists. The number of murders will increase in the coming years, as will the number of activists who will be criminalized, jailed, kidnapped, beaten, and threatened. As I write this, snipers with the Royal Canadian Mounted Police have been photographed with their rifles aimed at Indigenous people opposed to the expansion of the Trans Mountain Pipeline in British Columbia, Canada.

As the temperatures rise, so will the violence against those who dare to speak up and act to address climate change. For environmentalists, especially Indigenous activists, the consequences of climate change are very real, very painful, and very immediate. Indigenous people are on the front lines. They are dying in Amazonia, Central America, Africa, the Philippines, Australia, and Asia. In North America and Europe, they are being beaten and jailed. With opposition to the Dakota Access Pipeline, which impacts the Standing Rock Sioux Reservation in the United States, and opposition to the Coastal GasLink Pipeline that affects the Wet'suwet'en Nation in Canada, activists have been beaten, threatened, and arrested on their own land.

In Australia, my Sea Shepherd crew has teamed up with Aboriginal communities to fight the Adani coal mine and stop the plans to drill in the Great Australian Bight, an area more remote and with much harsher sea conditions than the Gulf of Mexico, where the Deepwater Horizon oil-spill disaster occurred. It's a

daunting and exhausting fight. We have already stopped BP,
Chevron, and the Norwegian company Equinor, but each victory
is followed by the emergence of a renewed challenge by a different corporation.

Another weapon in the corporate and government arsenal is
the criminalization of opposition, with courts siding against activists and the demonization of activists as ecoterrorists. I am actually
a victim of this, having been described as an ecoterrorist by the Jap-
anese government and charged with conspiracy to board a whaling
ship, an accusation by Japan that has had me placed on the Interpol
Red Notice list since 2012, thus restricting my travel outside the
United States. It was an acceptable sacrifice for me. We prevailed
in our efforts to force Japan's fleet of poachers from continuing
to illegally slaughter whales in the Southern Ocean Whale Sanctu-
ary. Recently, the British police placed Sea Shepherd, Greenpeace,
Extinction Rebellion, and other nonviolent groups that have not
broken any law on a terrorist watch list along with white suprem-
acist groups and jihadists.

Even when the media does not ignore activists, there often is an obvious bias in the reporting. The words "extremist," "militant," "fanatical," and "ill informed" are frequently used, in addition to the offensive and accusatory "ecoterrorist." Statements are also distorted in many cases to instill a negative bias in the minds of the public. I frequently have had my comments taken out of context or deliberately misconstrued. For example, I once told a group of trappers in Canada that if they think they can ignore nature's laws, there would be consequences. This was reported as me having said, "If you think you can ignore what I'm saying, there will be consequences." Any media outlet that is owned by a corporation with interests in resource extraction or negative ecological outcomes cannot be trusted to be impartial.

In addition, we have seen the rise of powerful public relations firms that pump out a steady stream of anti-environmentalist propaganda. In some cases, such as in British Columbia, Canada, the same PR company (in this case, Burson-Marsteller) represented clients from government, corporations, and media while simultaneously allowing them to coordinate a powerful program to manipulate public sentiments. They believe that truth is simply a matter of perspective. To them, facts are irrelevant; what is important is what people *accept* as fact. Money buys power and control, and fossil fuel corporations have immense wealth that allows them to stifle dissent by smothering, denying, and distorting the truth.

> Climate change is a hoax invented by the Chinese.
>
> —*former US president Donald Trump*

In the United States, election to congress or to the presidency takes money, a great deal of money. There are three ways to get that money. The first is the populist approach (think of Bernie Sanders), which entails millions of citizens making small donations. The second is dependence on huge corporations like the fossil fuel, tech, and pharmaceutical industries that pump hundreds of millions of dollars into elections and expect favors in return. The third is the rise of a billionaire class that can purchase power for themselves as individuals (think of people like Donald Trump or Michael Bloomberg) and whose allegiance is only to themselves and their friends. This is a trend we are seeing in recent elections in Australia, Brazil, and the United Kingdom, for example. Instead of government representing the citizenry, it has become government by the corporations, of the corporations, and for the corporations.

A few years ago, Princeton University published a position paper stating that the United States was no longer a democracy but instead an oligarchy. To be specific, I have called it an "oil-ocratic" oligarchy. Such an oligarchic dictatorship has long been in place in Russia and China.

For the most part, we the people go along with this control because we feel powerless and frightened, and, in many cases, we simply opt to remain uninformed and apathetic. In this new order, the people are simply a crop to be raised for only two purposes: to consume resources and to pay taxes. We are no longer people but sheeple, and taxes are how the sheep are shorn. Governments and their corporate masters demand obedience, docility, and ignorance in return for a false sense of security, material comforts, and enter-

tainment. Every few years the sheeple are given a couple of limited choices to perpetuate the illusion that they are in control so that they never feel the need to look up and see reality.

Fortunately, within the flock there are always a few black sheep, the ones that refuse to be subservient, that question authority, and that are motivated to challenge the entrenched status quo. These are the troublemakers who protest with their pens, cameras, skills, experience, and bodies. They are the same type of people who once freed the slaves, enfranchised women, and fought for civil rights. Today, they champion rights for animals and for nature. These are the sheep who look up.

Be Prepared

For decades, humanity had the opportunity to constructively address climate change but chose not to. Now that ship has sailed and is no longer an option. Radical legal regulations and lifestyle modifications would certainly help to mitigate the negative consequences of climate change, but there is a complete lack of economic and political motivation to take the threat seriously.

The Green New Deal was an option in the United States, but recent elections have demonstrated that the general public is not truly interested in backing a political solution. The sentiment is to retreat to the security of the past. There is a paucity of courage to face the obstacles coming at us from the future.

As I mentioned on page 13, we live in a society of addicts. Our collective addiction to fossil fuels and, more directly, to the material comforts of a fossil-fuel-driven world is seemingly impossible to shake off. Addicts don't want help. They want only one thing: a fix! We want our oil, our machines, our entertainment, and our self-indulgent materialistic lifestyles. We don't want to hear any doomsday scenarios or negative points of view that could dissolve our anthropocentric illusions. And we seem willing to pay for all of this with our submission to extinction.

Ironically, what will kill us may ultimately be what will save us. No species can survive outside of the three basic laws of ecology:

1. **The law of diversity:** An ecosystem requires diversity to survive and flourish. The greater the diversity, the stronger the system.

2. **The law of interdependence:** All species are dependent on all other species. The less diversity there is, the less interdependence there is.

3. **The law of finite resources:** There are limits to growth and to carrying capacity. When one species steals carrying capacity from other species, it diminishes diversity and interdependence.

Humans have stolen the great proportion of carrying capacity from ecosystems to feed and support our species and the relatively small number of animal and plant species that we have domesticated. Now we and these animals and plants dominate the majority of the planet's ecosystems and the collective biomass of humanity, and our domesticated slaves constitute a greater proportion of the planet than our wild flora and fauna.

Without the resources to support species diversity and interdependence, entire ecosystems will simply fall apart. Already coral reef systems worldwide are dying. Forest ecosystems have been destroyed. Acidification is impacting the seas. Wildfires are obliterating billions of creatures. New viruses are being unleashed. Yet humanity remains unmotivated, locked into economic, societal, and political mindsets that are so alienated from the natural order that we are oblivious to the unraveling of our life-support systems.

We believe that we are immune from the laws of ecology, that science will enable us, and that our religions will save us. We see what we desire to see. We hear what we wish to hear. And we will

not be persuaded to accept the reality that looms before us because ecological truths are not part of our collective belief system.

For humanity to survive, the entire socioeconomic and political structure of our civilization must crash. And it will. It's not a question of *if*; it's a question of *when*. And when it does, it will result in a combination of overpopulation, famine, drought, pandemics, environmental refugees, wars, and the diminishment of basic resources. All of these events will be enabled by the fact that humanity simply does not want to hear about them.

We just need to observe the worldwide reaction to the coronavirus to see how easily society panics. This virus is relatively minor compared to what is coming. We've already forgotten about the fires in Australia and the Amazon, and we don't see the connection. This crisis will pass and a new one will emerge, and then another and another. We will react to each one but not to the overall picture.

Climate change is the most serious threat to our survival that we have ever been faced with, yet we have chosen to simply ignore it as we continue our irrational obsessions with profits, wars, politics, and entertainment. Voices that speak out are knocked down and silenced and such persecutions will escalate. Truth is replaced with lies that are embraced without question.

Will some of us be prepared for collapse? Can we confront universal shortages in a world where global populations demand resources? Such a world will escalate environmental refugees, curtailment of human rights, and war.

We are good at war. We have spent thousands of years perfecting more efficient ways to destroy one another and justifying every atrocity in the name of patriotism, religion, and ideology. We do what we are told and kill who we are told to kill, and we do so believing that every action is honorable, ethical, and worthwhile. Our enemies are always the bad guys, and we, no matter who we are, are always the good guys from every perspective. The enemy, however, is us.

What is Extinction Rebellion? It is an effort to save ourselves from ourselves. We are so threatened by reality that we demonize any person who dares to speak the truth. And when people rise up to challenge the bastions of anthropocentrism, they are vilified, imprisoned, and murdered.

So what can we do? We can accept who we are and take steps to distance ourselves from collective human ignorance and arrogance. We can think for ourselves, question everything, and trust nothing.

The anthropocentric world is full of lies—lies that tell us what to eat, how to live, who to hate, who to respect, who to distrust, and who to trust. The airwaves are polluted with false information. They try to sell us peace, health, security, and material comfort, and all that is required in exchange is absolute acceptance of and submission to anthropocentric demands.

To shake off the shackles, we must no longer submit to believing what we are told to believe. Peace and security can be found through nature and by understanding that all species are interconnected. We are a part of the whole, not separate and dominant over it. This requires knowing who you are within the ecosystem in which you live in and knowing who your nonhuman neighbors are, understanding what they contribute to you, and acknowledging what you can contribute to them. It means being aware of what you eat and learning about the impact of such choices on the overall health of the environment. It means humbling yourself to accept that you are not more important than other species— *all* other species. It means not being concerned about criticism. My job as a biocentric conservationist is to say things many people do not want to hear and to do things that offend some people. I'm here to piss people off, to make waves, and to rock the boat (and sometimes to actually sink a boat or two). It means no longer holding allegiance to anthropocentric constructs. It means rejoining the natural world. For the biocentric, there are no borders, only relationships. With every decision, we must ask ourselves: Is this good for the planet, and if it's good for the planet, is it good for humanity?

These realizations came to me from a deep, personal connection with a dying sperm whale. At that moment, I saw what we humans are, and I was repulsed by that perception. I knew then that protecting and defending this whale and his kind and all other nonhuman species was what I had to do.

In 1986, after my crew sank half the Icelandic whaling fleet, I was confronted by a former colleague from my Greenpeace days who told me our actions were an embarrassment to Greenpeace and the movement. "What you did was criminal, reprehensible,

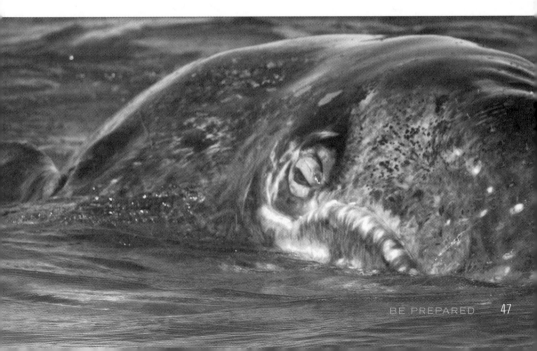

and immoral, and it has caused great harm to our movement," he told me.

I replied, "We did not sink those whale-killing ships for you, for Greenpeace, or for any movement. We sank them for the whales. If you can find me just one whale that disagrees with that action, I will promise to never do it again."

"That's ridiculous," he said.

"Perhaps, but that is what it is. The whales are our clients, not people."

By embracing biocentrism, I discovered a feeling of immense freedom; I was free to think. I also discovered that I had little fear of anything, and that was the greatest feeling of all. It was liberating. I understood that death is very much a part of life and that the inevitability of death is absolute. Acceptance of death is the rejection of all fear: fear of speaking, fear of acting, fear of being ourselves.

If I should fear anything, however, it should be climate change and the increasing diminishment of biodiversity. These are threats that will have consequences for me personally, but that is unimportant. What is significant are the consequences for the future of all life on our planet, including the lives of our children.

Extinction troubles me greatly. The loss of every species diminishes the biosphere, and thus it diminishes us all. I fear for the survival of a million species, and that includes our own.

My son, my daughter, my grandchildren, and all our grandchildren, are on a collision course with the collective consequences of the ecological sins of our species. I am often asked why, if I fear for the future, did I father two children. It's a valid question, and it has brought accusations of hypocrisy against me. That, in itself, does not bother me; we are all hypocrites. We were born into hypocrisy. Our hypocrisy is evident in the foods we eat, the cars we drive, the clothing we wear, and in pretty much every aspect of our behavior. But it remains a valid question nonetheless.

The reason that I had children is because I need teachers, and children are the greatest of teachers. I need to see the world through their eyes because, if I cannot, I simply would not have hope, inspiration, and motivation. When I have been asked what we should teach our children, I have always said that we need to teach them very little. We can guide them, but more importantly, we need to listen to them. They have the intuition, the innocence, and the imagination to perceive the world as it is and not as what we want it to be.

When I was a child, I cut up a map of the world and brought the continents together. I told my teacher that I thought there was once one big continent. She told me that this idea was ridiculous. Yet I was right. Why had I thought that? Because it simply made sense. I also said that I thought dinosaurs were birds, were warm blooded, and probably had feathers. I was told that it was a cute idea but wrong. Yet, again, I was right.

In 1975, I had the opportunity to speak to a school in Haida Gwaii. All the children were Haida, and the morning began with a talk to the lower grades. My first question was how many of them spoke Haida. They all did. My second question was what did they know about whales. I said nothing more as they told me about the whales they had seen and all the stories they had been told by their elders.

Later in the morning, I spoke to the middle school, where about half the kids spoke Haida and knew less about whales than the younger students. In the afternoon, I spoke to the seniors at the high school, where only a couple of them spoke Haida and not one seemed to know or care about whales. I was stunned. This Canadian school in Haida Gwaii had taken these wonderfully bright, intelligent kids, removed their intuition and imaginations, and filled them full of rationality and logic, transforming them from what they naturally were to what the education system demanded: subjugation to anthropocentrism.

My critics say the world needs fewer children. I believe the world needs more *real* children. We need their vision, their instincts, their intuition, and their imagination. What we don't need are post-natal abortions, wherein all the children are irresponsibly brought into this world without love, nurturing, compassion, and education. We abuse them and they grow up to abuse others. We diminish them and they grow up to diminish others. Children are seeds, and seeds dropped into poor, rocky soil will not grow into healthy plants.

I listen to my son. I share and encourage his imaginary world. When he tells me that he talks to animals, I believe him. When he tells me that he wants to go to Mars, I say, "Why not! You can be whatever you wish to be."

He will, of course, discover that there are boundaries and limitations, but it is not for me to tell him that he can't attempt to challenge limitations. I want him to find the possible solutions to seemingly impossible problems, and that can only be done by encouraging his passion, courage, and imagination.

It's not for me to tell him to love nature. Nature is there for him to discover, and I help him find the paths he is looking for. By respecting nature myself, I provide an example. By respecting women, I encourage him to do the same. By being kind to animals, I set the stage for him to do so also.

My hopes for his future are not demands. The most challenging task, however, is to explain that his future may be a difficult one and to provide some guidance going forward. The most important thing that I can contribute is to demonstrate that one person has the power to change the world. He will need that confidence most of all—the confidence to remain immune to negativity and nonconstructive criticism. He will also need the confidence to never submit to the demands of any person or group.

8

Wilderness

One key to survival is a willingness to embrace true wilderness. My favorite place on this planet is Antarctica. It is the last place on Earth where humans are not dominant over most of the continent. Between 2002 and 2013, I spent a total of three years of my life on the waters surrounding the Antarctic continent or upon the icy terrain itself. And I loved every moment there: the penguins, the leopard seals, the whales, the incredibly huge icebergs and glaciers, the magnificent expanse of the Ross Ice Shelf, and the inspiring isolation of Scott Island and the Bay of Whales. What most people see as a harsh and hostile wasteland, I saw as an inspiring panoramic landscape of rugged beauty and a wondrous haven for nonhuman life. It was a true wilderness—isolated, stark, and dominated by a biocentric interdependent diversity of life.

That is also why I have always been drawn to the sea and its seemingly lifeless desert of waves and wind and the wilderness of miles

and miles of water, water, and more water. Beneath the seeming barrenness of the surface lies a cornucopia of rich and vibrant diversity.

Henry David Thoreau once wrote: "In wildness is the preservation of the world." But it is more than that. Wildness, or wilderness, is the preservation of the very essence of what we are. When wilderness is diminished, we also are diminished. And should wilderness disappear, we shall also disappear.

Today most people are quite alienated from wilderness. In fact, more and more people have no idea just what it is. I have heard wilderness described as the place where there is no Wi-Fi or cell phone accessibility, something I find quite sad and even difficult to comprehend. Some people have been reported to actually panic when they find themselves in the "wilderness" of no electronic reception.

I suppose it's understandable. We have now seen an entire generation that has been raised on cell phones and the internet. They have never experienced a world without social networks and mobile phones. This dependency on technology has made society a much more lonely place, as the gadgets tend to isolate us from each other. The ultimate absurdity is two people texting each other while they're in the same room, experiencing each other and reality on tiny screens.

I don't think there is anything more symbolic of our alienation from nature than the ridiculous game of golf. Large tracts of wildland are appropriated and converted into something totally domesticated for the sole purpose of amusing people with a stick and a ball. Bushes are knocked down and undesirable plants are poisoned, only to be replaced by manicured, genetically modified green grass and barren tiny deserts of sand, devoid of life. The acreage is bombarded with herbicides, pesticides, fungicides, and chemical fertilizers. The bees are poisoned to prevent stings and possible allergic reactions, and the soil is poisoned to prevent moles, gophers, rabbits, and other species from making themselves at home. It's a declaration that this ground belongs only to the people who own and control it, and it exists for their pleasure alone. When I see a golf course, I see a proclamation that humanity demands total subjugation of nature, and that we will own and sterilize wilderness as an exercise in anthropocentric superiority. It iterates that our society has a grotesque tendency toward the egocentric. Everything we do is for ourselves: our comfort, our safety, our pleasure. We have taught our youth to define something as critical, vast, complex, and beautiful as wilderness only in relation to themselves. Then, narrowing the vision even further, it's visible only through the lens of technological man-made inventions. That is what we are most proud of.

Grizzly bear defender Doug Peacock once gave a speech on the importance of big, dangerous animals that can eat a person. Such creatures remind us that we are not all-powerful and that we need to be humble.

Many years ago, a friend of mine, Timothy Treadwell, and his girlfriend, Amie Huguenard, were killed by a grizzly bear, and I remember some media reporting on how tragic it was that they died so unnaturally. Yet being killed by a bear or slain by a shark is far more natural than dying in an automobile accident or being shot by another human being. Tim lived with grizzly bears for thirteen years without injury, and during that time he learned a great deal about them. He learned to appreciate them and to recognize their value. In fact, they gave meaning to his life. He once told me that he fully expected to be killed by a bear, and, if he was, his only regret would be if the bear was slain because of it.

Some critics said that he was foolish for living with the bears, but the truth was that he was dying in the city from drugs and depression. His bears gave him thirteen years of happiness and joy, and he died doing what he loved to do. The bear that killed him was not one of the bears he had been observing for years. He was killed by a bear that was wounded by a poacher and was not a resident of the area Tim was studying.

Each and every time that I have taken a ship into the Southern Ocean, I have felt truly alive. The ice, the storms, and the temperatures energized me, and I never once felt fear or discomfort from the elements. I can't imagine how hollow I would feel if I didn't have my travels, explorations, confrontations, and discoveries. I have needed and still need wilderness and adventure; I will always need them.

Most people are threatened by uncertainty and insecurity. Because of this, we have eradicated predators, exterminated wildlife, and cut down forests. Big, fierce animals threaten us and make us feel inferior because of our desire to dominate nature. For many people, wilderness has been something to subdue or destroy. Big game hunters, for example, are exceptionally insecure people. They need to kill in order to feel validated, strong, and superior. It is fear that motivates them. Without their big guns, they know they would be embarrassingly inadequate and puny in comparison to the noble creatures they mercilessly murder.

It is appropriate that this sixth mass extinction is called the Anthropocene. It is our anthropocentric illusions that enable our destructive behavior. Anthropocentric values negate anything that is not human. Through the lens of anthropocentricity, animals and plants are to be used any which way we desire: for food, for labor, or simply for amusement. We cannot, in fact, we should not survive unless we learn to appreciate and to live with other species. Our survival lies in embracing biocentrism, the understanding that we are a part of nature and not dominant over nature. Our failure to recognize interconnectedness is killing us. When we diminish an ecosystem, we diminish ourselves.

Once, when I was speaking at the University of Texas, a young student seemed offended by my presentation on biocentrism. He told me that we do not really need animals other than the ones we eat because we have technology, and that we don't need to be interdependent with any other species of animal. He said that Jesus Christ is all we need because only God gives us life.

I looked straight at him, and here is what I said:

Do you know what I see when I look at you? You think that you are just you, all independent and proud, yet right now, a great part of you is not even you. You are a symbiont, a community of billions of bacteria, in and on your body. In fact, it is just as much their body as yours, because without the thousands of bacterial species that share your existence, you could not digest your food, clean your skin, or even groom your eyebrows. In short, without all those creatures, you would be stone-cold dead. And outside of your body, the bees pollinate the fruit you eat, the worms provide the soil to grow your vegetables, the insects help to clean up your waste, and the trees and the phytoplankton manufacture the oxygen that keeps you alive. Without all these things, this anthropocentric fabrication you call Jesus won't be much help in keeping you alive.

Anthropocentrism defines our values, and those values are always 100 percent material, human-oriented values. Imagine walking into the city of Mecca and spitting on the Black Stone. You would be ripped to pieces by angry Muslims. Imagine walking up to the Wailing Wall in Jerusalem with a pickax to break up the stones. You would most likely get an Israeli bullet in the back. Or imagine entering the Vatican and taking a hammer to Michelangelo's *Pietà*. You would no doubt be heading to prison quite quickly.

These places are sacred to anthropocentric values, and any attack on these material objects is considered blasphemy. Yet each and every day we destroy the most mysterious, most beautiful, and most sacred cathedrals of nature—the rainforests of Amazonia and the Great Barrier Reef of Australia—without any consequences for the destroyer. Such people are called loggers and businesspeople.

The best explanation that I have ever heard to describe our anthropocentric values was from a ranger in Zimbabwe who had shot and killed a poacher that was about to kill an endangered rhinoceros. Human rights groups had vilified him. How dare he take a human life to protect an animal! His response was that if he had been a policeman in Harare, and a man had run out of Barclays Bank with a bag of paper money, and he had shot the man in the back and killed him right there on the street, he would be called a hero and most likely would be given a medal. "How is it," he asked, "that a bag of paper is worth more than the future heritage of the nation of Zimbabwe?"

When I was teaching at ArtCenter College of Design in Pasadena, California, in the nineties, I asked my students to take a notebook and list all the nonhuman living things they saw that week. At the end of the week, a few had listed cats, dogs, pigeons, and butterflies. One young lady, however, had armed herself with a field guide to plants and animals in Southern California and had a long list that included insects, plants, trees, numerous birds, mushrooms, a rattlesnake, raccoons, and many other species. She saw what was around her when most of the students saw nothing. I gave her an A+.

Wilderness allows us to see, feel, smell, and hear the great community of life and to understand that we humans must be a part of that community. When we can't even see the natural world around us, it is very easy to abuse it. Most people can identify more company logos than they can identify species of plants and animals.

In order to defend and protect the natural world, we need to feel the sand beneath our bare feet. We need to experience the coldness of a mountain stream. We need to feel salt spray from the ocean on our faces. We need to experience the smell of the forest. And we need to be humbled by the sight of an eagle, a bear, a whale, or a tiger. We need to embrace the humility of a world larger than ourselves. We also need to experience uncertainty, insecurity, and fear, and in doing so, understand the value of such emotions.

We need to discover who we are, and when we do, when we reject the yoke of anthropocentric dogma, we can discover the true meaning of the word "freedom." Domination is not freedom. Freedom is belonging, being a part of something large, real, and complete.

Climate Change Stress

I am reading about and hearing from many people who feel trauma-
tized and depressed by climate change and who feel stressed and
frightened by the COVID-19 virus. For a great number of people,
ignorance is bliss. But for climate scientists, activists, doctors, and
intelligent people in general, the reality of climate change and pandemics
can be quite depressing. They realize that stopping the rising global levels of greenhouse gases is practically impossible and that there will be
real and potentially (almost certainly) catastrophic consequences. This
is like being told you are going to die from cancer and
there is no cure.

I have spoken to children with terminal cancer
and many accept their fate quietly and with
great strength. They still love their family and
their pets and feel a deep appreciation for the
gift of life they have experienced. It's been my
observation that children accept death with
less stress than adults.

I am often asked how I deal with stress,
considering the nature of my work and the numer-

ous death threats and legal challenges I've faced, not to mention the many dangerous campaigns that we undertake. For me, the answer is simple: I don't deal with stress because I tend to not suffer from stress. Following are the ten primary reasons why, and for anyone suffering from anxiety, worry, or stress, this is my advice:

1. Climate change is what it is. Whatever the issue, whatever the threat, whatever the circumstances, it simply is what it is. Stressing will not change the situation. The solution may seem impossible, but stress is not the answer. To solve an impossible problem, we need to use our imagination, passion, and courage to discover the possible solution. And if we can't, at least we tried, and the time to stop trying is when we die.

2. "It's always something." I say this all the time to my crews whenever a problem arises. "It's always something. And if it's not something, it's something else. But it's always something." This means that life comes with obstacles, challenges, and problems. Problems should not be unexpected; they are inevitable. All problems can be dealt with by dealing with them, delegating someone else to deal with them, or ignoring them. One thing for sure, on a ship it is definitely always something. Right now, on planet Earth, that something is climate change.

3. Stay calm. There really is nothing worth getting upset about. I have found in the numerous life-and-death circumstances I have experienced that it was my lack of stress that pulled me through. Once, while I was diving, my regulator jammed at thirty meters. I calmly signaled my partner to indicate my situation. Panicking will not save your life. If you lose something, fretting about it will not recover the object. Anger emanates from stress. Without stress, there can be no anger. Without stress, there is an absence of panic. Without stress, there is little fear.

4. Nothing material is permanent; therefore, objects are not worth stressing about. Your car gets damaged, something you own gets stolen, or you lose your investments; none of these is really important. Material objects and comforts are nice, but they should not be anchors keeping you attached to stress. Move on.

5. Friends are friends . . . or they are not. A true friend will never betray you, and if a "friend" does betray you, then he or she is simply not a friend. Always walk away from betrayal and do not stress about it. True and loyal friends are rare treasures and should be treated as such. Loyalty begets loyalty. Compassion begets compassion. Courage begets courage. You can only control your own loyalty, compassion, and courage, not those of others. And if others prove that they're disloyal or they betray you, the treasure is no longer a treasure but merely a bauble to be tossed aside. Never stress about betrayal or loss. It is what it is.

6. Loneliness is an opportunity to discover yourself. You can't find someone to love you if you don't first love yourself. The secret to finding the right person is to not look for that person. Love should blossom from the ground like a lovely wildflower; it can't be cultivated until after it is realized. Do not seek the seed, but let the flower reveal an opportunity for you to grow and learn.

7. Relationships are like streams, constantly flowing. And as they flow, they meet obstacles. Some are minor and others are major, but a relationship either flows around the obstacle or it is blocked. If it is permanently blocked, it ends. This is not cause for stress, angry resentment, or envy. It is what it is. Move on with appreciation and without bitterness for the relationship that is no more, and open your heart to other possibilities that life presents. The most important factor in maintaining a meaningful relationship with lovers, family, or friends is simply acceptance. You need to accept them for who they are, and they need to accept you for who you are. If you can't accept another person for who they are, you need to stop inflicting stress on that person and walk away. And if another person does not accept you for who you are, you need to walk away, regardless of the nature of the relationship. Stress kills, and living with a person who does not accept you for who you are is like living with a person who is slowly killing you.

8. Fear is a poison that seeps into the soul and paralyzes our senses, generating paranoia, insecurity, and anger. Try to not let fear enter your life. There is really little to fear because things are what they are and will be what they will be. Remember, you are the captain of your fate and the master of your soul and body. Who you are and what you wish to be depend on you and you alone. A person free of fear can accomplish far more than a person shackled to fear.

9. Oscar Wilde once said, "There is only one thing in the world worse than being talked about, and that is not being talked about." People talk. They gossip. They make false accusations. Some enjoy insulting and belittling others. They are easily dealt with by ignoring them. Responding to them is what they want, so don't respond. Reacting to them is what they want, so don't react. Such people are not worthy of causing stress to you. They come from a place of insecurity, envy, and fear. It is their stress, and their stress is their problem. It should not be yours. Climate change deniers just need to be ignored. Time is too valuable to waste on arguing or debating with people who deny reality.

10. Do not fear death. Stand firm for what you believe in, fight against all odds, and never surrender. The one absolute of life is death. We all will die. What matters is not dying but living. It is how you live that is important, and the only thing important about dying is how you die. It should be a death without fear and with dignity and acceptance that it is what it is. The person without fear dies but once; the person shackled by fear dies slowly from stress and anxiety. Accept the inevitable, embrace the final reality of life, and smile in the face of the infinite. The real secret to happiness is to not fear your own death, to not fear failure or ridicule, and to not fear others.

Stress is an obstacle to mindfulness and an impediment to impeccability. Stress is the cause of migraines, cancer, and many other ailments. It is the reason people smoke, take drugs, and drink excessively. People often ask me why I've never smoked anything; the reason is that I have never felt inclined to do so. It never seemed healthy to me, and I have always been mindful of the consequences. I think stress blocks mindfulness of consequences. The same holds true for getting drunk or stoned. Without stress, there is no need or desire to do either.

Mindfulness is simply the awareness of who you are and what you are doing. A person who is mindful is a person free of stress. Unfulfilled desire leads to stress. Wanting nothing allows you to appreciate what you have. When you want nothing, you want for nothing. We all have basic needs for food, warmth, shelter, clothing, and companionship. Mindfulness allows us to be secure with our basic needs. Everything else is a luxury, and although luxuries may be appreciated, we should not depend on them. Depending on luxuries leads to stress.

I have never worked a day in my life for the sole purpose of making money. I have never wanted to own anything. Although I do own property and material things now, I do not allow those things to own me. I never engage in arguments about money or debts. I tend to avoid debts, but when debts occur, my position is that they are what they are, and they're certainly not something to be troubled about.

As far as basic needs, I learned to address this as a teenager when I left home at the age of fifteen. I had no money, no place to stay, no prospects. I jumped a freight train and rode in the automobiles being transported from Toronto all the way to Vancouver. I arrived and camped in the abandoned gun towers on Wreck Beach, and the first thing I did was go to Vancouver Community College to enroll. I found a job, moved out of the gun tower into a single room that I rented, and went from there. Looking back, I see it as an adventure. I had nothing, but there was no stress. I simply replaced the insecurity of my position with an adventurous experience. I treated every job as a learning experience. I was employed as a longshore worker, teamster, tree planter, warehouse laborer, short order cook, baker, painter, carpet layer, postal carrier, tour guide, landscaper, and seafarer. All were educational experiences.

The truth is that all of life is an adventure: the good and the bad, the ups and the downs, the experiences, the hardships, the thrills, and the times that are lonely, happy, or difficult. Even the loss of friends and family can be dealt with by acknowledging that death is what it is. It is inevitable, and although we may sincerely mourn, we can do so without being stressed. This may be difficult to understand, but it is indeed quite possible. With the passing of every friend, with the passing of my brother, I have silently said goodbye, along with the appreciation of having known them.

I have gone into situations many times where the risk of injury, death, or imprisonment was practically a certainty. My approach has always been one of acceptance. And, amazingly, I am still alive and still free. When I have had nothing, I have had everything I need; and when I have risked all, I have usually been successful.

I am not infallible; I have made mistakes in my life, many of them. I have at times in the past responded with anger, although it's mostly been limited to the poison of the pen and rarely has been physical. I have let some people down and missed opportunities. But the one thing I have been able to do in my life is avoid stress.

I am seventy years old as I write this, and I am healthy, happy, and optimistic. As a father of a four-year-old boy, I am as passionate and active as I ever have been, even more so because I have had the grace of experience and the satisfaction of achievement in the areas I chose to address.

Do not let stress ruin your health, your love, or your life. Dread nothing and live the adventure that is life. It may well be the only life you will ever have. Even if you believe in an afterlife (and don't stress about that, either), the fact is, you will never be able to confirm its existence, so there's no sense wasting the unique life that you have right now. A stress-free life is not only possible, it's essential for your health and happiness.

How do I deal with the reality of climate change? First, I accept it. I see the seriousness of it, and I can visualize the consequences. Second, I am an activist. I work to mitigate the consequences and help people educate others about the issues and threats. Third, I look at the big picture.

A few thousand environmental activists have been murdered over the last two decades. I intend to honor their work and memories by continuing to defend this planet as passionately and courageously as I can. Surrendering to hopelessness is not demonstrating appreciation for their sacrifices.

There have been five previous major mass extinctions in the history of the planet. The Anthropocene is the sixth event. What I have learned is that it takes an average of eighteen million years to fully recover from an extinction event. That is a relatively small period of time for the planet. It means that all the damage we have done will be repaired, and eighteen million years from now, Earth will be a very nice and beautiful place again. This may not mean much to many people, but the thought always brings a smile to my face. Remember, no matter what we do, even if we should fail, all is not lost for planet Ocean.

What Can We Do?

Most people know about the things we should do to mitigate climate change: Don't eat meat or fish, become a vegan or vegetarian, don't fly in planes, don't drive a car, don't use fossil fuels, don't use plastic, consume less, plant trees, don't have children, and many other things. Some of these are easily doable, some are difficult, and some are very impractical. But to be perfectly honest, none of these actions will prevent climate change from becoming a greater and greater threat. The genie is out of the bottle.

I admit that there have been very worthy efforts. The rise of plant-based foods has been quite successful, and the number of vegans and vegetarians increase each year. There have been exciting inventions to sequester carbon and advances in developing alternatives to plastic. There are beach cleanups, conferences and more conferences, meetings, Ted Talks, climate strikes, and a very huge increase in green content, also known as greenwashing. And, of course, we are far more aware now than ever before in our history. The number of climate activists, however, is still a relatively small minority of our population and will remain so unless humanity disavows the prevailing paradigm of anthropocentrism.

Human societies are controlled by anthropocentric governments, whether they are left, right, or centrist, or communist, socialist, or fascist. Every economic system focuses on growth, production, exploitation, and consumerism. There is not a single national government that views the preservation of nature as its priority. There is not a single government that is willing to forsake war and nationalism. But unless governments take real action, unless fossil fuel industries are dismantled, unless environmental laws are actually enforced, all the initiatives advanced by activists will accomplish very little.

Another addiction humans have is this thing called jobs. Politicians are very fearful of anything that causes job loss unless it is in the interest of the corporations for people to lose their jobs. Loggers or miners laid off because of an endangered species is unacceptable, but people losing their jobs to benefit shareholders is commonplace and acceptable.

Biocentrism means casting off national identities, not participating in wars, and rejecting the economics of resource extraction. Survival in the Anthropocene is really an adaptation to a new reality. It is accepting the seriousness of climate change and developing a new attitude of acceptance and adaptability.

A GREEN UTOPIA

A green utopia can only become a reality if the following are implemented now or in the very near future.

1. Ending dependence on all fossil fuels and utilizing alternative energy sources.
2. Dismantling the war machines.
3. Adopting plant-based diets universally.
4. Enacting a hundred-year moratorium on commercial fishing to allow the seas to recover from the damage we have inflicted.

5. Increasing global biodiversity.

6. Stopping the logging of old growth and rainforests.

7. Engaging in serious tree-planting and rewilding campaigns to restore biodiversity.

8. Ceasing the production of all single-use plastics.

9. Discouraging overpopulation through education, allowing women to have abortions upon request, and providing easy access to proper family planning.

10. Removing corporate and government control over all mainstream media.

Under the current political, economic, and philosophical perspectives, the chances of any of these solutions being implemented is zero. Nature, however, is giving us a hint that some of these things will be involuntarily enforced regardless. The COVID-19 virus has slowed down economic systems and industrialized activities. In just a very short time, we have witnessed the cleansing of the atmosphere and waterways, the shuttering of wet markets, and the growing awareness that we as a species have created problems that we must resolve.

THE GREEN DILEMMA

We are faced with the quandary of how to survive climate change in a world in which governments, corporations, and media have elected to be irresponsible. Although we may not be able to control the decisions those entities make, we can control our own choices. We can decide to embark on lifestyles with lower carbon footprints and pledge to become activists. What kind of activists? That is something each individual must determine. We need to assess our own skills and abilities and resolve to do what we can, given our unique talents.

The strength of an ecosystem lies in diversity and interdependence. Within a movement, diverse approaches include education, litigation, legislation, intervention, and various levels of activism, including civil disobedience. While these actions may at times seem futile, I take inspiration from knowing that the majority of positive social movements haven't arisen overnight and were fueled by dedicated, passionate people. This has included people like Mahatma Gandhi in India, William Wilberforce in England, and Frederick Douglass in the United States in their efforts to end slavery; Dr. Martin Luther King Jr. and the US civil rights movement; and the suffragettes and their global victories to enfranchise women. By modeling the most commendable human traits, the leaders of these movements have taught me patience, persistence, passion, and courage.

One of the most valuable lessons I ever received was from American Indian Movement (AIM) leader Russell Means. It was in March 1973. I was twenty-two and a volunteer medic for AIM during the occupation of Wounded Knee in South Dakota. We were under siege, surrounded by three thousand US federal officers and troops. They were shooting into the village every night, and the assault wounded forty-six Native Americans and killed two. During this conflict, Russell Means remained strong and confident, despite the odds being so much against us. I asked him directly why were we holding on when we had no chance of winning and the opposition was so much stronger.

He smiled and calmly said, "We're not concerned about the odds against us. We're not concerned about winning or losing. We're here because this is where we need to be. This is the time we need to be here, and this is the right thing for us to do. We can't be concerned about the consequences. We act today, and that will define what the future will be."

We stand strong today because we are doing what is right.

The movement to address climate change may be a losing cause, but losing causes are the best ones to fight for because they are where possible solutions for seemingly impossible problems can be found. We only need to look at the impossible odds that women had to overcome to secure the right to vote or the odds that slavery could be abolished. Humans tend to be strongest when the obstacles are daunting and victory is hard to fathom.

The best advice I can give anyone involved in this movement is to act today with courage and passion. Be patient and let each day and each effort define the future. Each and every one of us has the power to change the world, and that is a fact forged in the trials of history.

The Green New Deal

The most visionary and progressive political approach has been the Green New Deal, a proposal to address climate change and economic inequality through legislation in the United States. It is a pair of resolutions sponsored by Representative Alexandria Ocasio-Cortez (D-NY) and Senator Edward Markey (D-MA). It failed to pass but was championed by US presidential candidate Bernie Sanders and opposed by then presidential candidate Joe Biden.

Extinction Rebellion

In 2018, Roger Hallam and Gail Bradbrook founded Extinction Rebellion in Great Britain. Their objective was to create a nonviolent civil disobedience movement in an effort to motivate governments to address climate change. The movement is now global.

Extinction Rebellion's website states the following aims:

1. Government must tell the truth by declaring a climate and ecological emergency, working with other institutions to communicate the urgency for change.
2. Government must act now to halt biodiversity loss and reduce greenhouse gas emissions to net zero by 2025.
3. Government must create and be led by the decisions of a Citizens' Assembly on climate and ecological justice.

350.Org

Founded in 2007 by Bill McKibben, 350.org is an international organization addressing the climate crisis. Its stated goal is to end the use of fossil fuels and transition to renewable energy by building a global grassroots movement. The "350" in the name stands for 350 ppm (parts per million) of carbon dioxide, which has been identified as the safe upper limit to avoid a climate tipping point. As of today, the current level has reached 415 ppm. Through online campaigns, grassroots organizing, mass public actions, and collaboration with an extensive network of partner groups and organizations, 350.org has mobilized thousands of volunteer organizers in over 188 countries.

School Strike for Climate (Skolstrejk för klimatet)

School Strike for Climate was founded in 2018 by Swedish teenager Greta Thunberg. She has demonstrated that youth is not an obstacle in expressing concern, direction, and outrage. Since 2018, Thunberg has confronted world leaders and organized climate strikes with millions of participants around the world.

Sea Shepherd Conservation Society

In 1977, I founded Sea Shepherd Conservation Society for the purpose of defending marine biodiversity. We do this by stopping poachers, cleaning beaches, advocating a vegan lifestyle, and constantly and patiently promoting the fact that if the ocean dies, we all die!

I have also spent a lifetime promoting biocentrism and the understanding that, to survive, we must live in harmony with all other species and in accordance with the laws of ecology.

CONCLUSION

Growth for the sake of growth is a form of behavior that humans share with cancer cells. It is an indefensible delusion that will destroy civilization, as it diminishes the very life-support system that sustains us. Survival for humanity in the age of climate change can only be achieved by rejecting anthropocentric ideologies and adapting to a biocentric lifestyle that embraces the importance of interdependence and diversity and acknowledges and respects the reality of finite resources. This, along with our passion for life, our courage in facing obstacles, and our efforts through imagination and resourcefulness, will be our salvation as a species. I am committed to finding possible solutions to seemingly impossible obstacles like climate change. The fact is, we have no other choice.

INDEX

our survival dependent on, 57
Sea Shepherd Conservation Society
and, 75
biodiversity
defending marine, 75
Extinction Rebellion's goals on, 74
increasing and restoring, 71
threat of diminishment of, 48
bleaching, of coral, 16, 26
Bloomberg, Michael, 39–40
BP, 38
Bradbrook, Gail, 74
Brazil, government's allegiance to
corporations in, 40
British Columbia, Canada, 1, 37, 39
Bunker C oil, 19
Burson-Marsteller, 39
bush fires, 8, 27

C

Cáceres, Berta, 36
California
ArtCenter College of Design, 58
fires in, 8–9
stopping Soviet whaling fleet off
the coast of, 2
Canada
anti-environmentalist propaganda
in, 39
Coastal GasLink Pipeline, 37
Trans Mountain Pipeline in, 37
Wet'suwet'en Nation in, 37
Canadian Coast Guard weather
ships, 1
Canberra, 9
carbon emissions/carbon dioxide. see
also greenhouse gas emissions
acid rain and, 26
from bush and forest fires, 27
from cruise ships, 19
in Earth's life-support system, 26,
32
increase in, 18, 27
Permian-Triassic mass extinction
and, 24, 27

source of, 17–18
stabilized with oxygen, 24
cargo aircraft, 19
chemical fertilizers, 33, 55
Chevron, 38
children, 49–51, 50–51, 61
China
military aircraft of, 19
oil consumption in, 15
oligarchy in, 40
Citizens' Assembly, 74
civil disobedience, 72
climate activists. See environmental
activists/activism
climate change
Antarctica temperatures, 7
causing mass extinctions from
the past, 23–25
coral reefs and, 16–17
emergence of new viruses from,
11
finding solutions to, 21
future generations and, 7–8
green utopia and, 70–71
how author deals with reality of,
67
ignoring the warnings of, 10–11,
44–45
impact of, 26–27
Pandora's box of, 9–10
Permian-Triassic extinction event
and, 23–24
stress from, 61–67
ways of addressing, 10, 69–71
climate change activism. See environmental activists/activism
coal deposits, prolonged burning of,
24
Coastal GasLink Pipeline, 37
commercial airlines, 18, 19
commercial fishing, 70
commercial fishing, moratorium on,
70
coral bleaching, 16, 26
coral reefs, 16–17

corporations
    denial of climate change by CEOs
        of, 11
    extraction-industry, 35
    fossil fuel, 39
    government's relationship with,
        39–40
    public relations propaganda, 40
    sheeples submitting to power of,
        40–41
Costa Rica, 36
COVID-19 virus/pandemic
    cruise ships and, 19–20
    future threats and, 45
    slowing economic systems, 72
    stress and, 61
Cretaceous-Tertiary extinction, 17, 25
crop failures, 16
cruise ships, 19–20

D

Dakota Access Pipeline, 37
Dalniy Vostok (ship), 5
dead zones, in the ocean, 20
death, 65
    acceptance of, 48, 61
    inevitability of, 66
    not fearing your, 65
death threats, 61–62
Deepwater Horizon oil-spill disas-
    ter, 37
desertification, 27
dinosaurs, 25, 33, 49
diversity, law of, 44
domestic animals
    fish fed, 20
    raised for meat, 20
    stopping mass slaughter of, 10
Douglass, Frederick, 72
drought, 27, 45
dust storms, 9

E

Earth
    life beginning on, 25–26

mass extinctions on, 23–27
"spaceship" analogy to, 31–32
as the water planet, 29–31
ecology, three basic laws of, 44
ecoterrorists, 38, 39
endangered species, job losses and, 70
environmental activists/activism
    assessing your skills for becoming,
        72
    biocentric, 47–48
    challenging the status quo, 41
    demonization and criminilization
        of, 38–39
    on impossible odds of winning,
        72–73
    indigenous, 35, 37
    media bias in reporting about, 39
    models from other social move-
        ments and, 72
    murder of, 35–37, 67
    organizations, 73–75
    propaganda by public relations
        firms, 39
    as small minority of population,
        70
environmental refugees, 45, 46
epidemics, 16
Equinor, 38
evolution, 25–26
exoskeletons in invertebrate species,
    weakening of, 26
extinction, 25. *see also* mass extinc-
    tions
    cruising toward, 19–20
    driving towards, 17–18
    eating our way toward our own,
        20
    emergence of new species and, 11
    flying towards, 18–19
    of humanity, 5
Extinction Rebellion, 38, 46, 74
extraction-industry corporations, 35

F

famine, 45

Holocene (Anthropocene) extinction
    era. *See* Anthropocene era
Honduras, 36
Huguenard, Amie, 55
human population
    decline in, 10, 15–16
    overpopulation, 15, 45, 71
human species
    addiction to oil, 13–15
    addressing climate change, 46–47,
        69–75
    alienated from wilderness, 54–55
    anthropocentric view of.*See* an-
        thropocentric view and values
    believing they are immune from
        laws of ecology, 44–45
    climate change and, 27, 33, 43
    dictatorship of our own species, 5
    enslavement of animals and
        plants by, 33
    experiencing the natural world,
        58–59
    as hosts for new viruses, 11
    in interdependent life-support sys-
        tem, 32
    Late Devonian event and, 25
    as passenger species, on "space-
        ship" Earth, 32
    stress in, 61–65
    threatened by big and dangerous
        animals, 56
humility, 55, 59
Hunter, Robert, 2–3, 9
hypocrisy, 14, 49

I
Icelandic whaling fleet, 47
ice, melting, 26, 27
ichthyostegalians, 25
India, military aircraft of, 19
Indian Ocean, 1
indigenous people
    murder of activists, 35–36, 37
    opposed to expansion of Trans
        Mountain Pipeline, 37

Wet'suewet'en Nation, 37
Wounded Knee occupation,
        South Dakota, 72–73
industrial fertilizers, 10
Industrial Revolution, 18, 27
infrastructure collapse, 16
insects, 23, 31, 58
interconnectedness and interdepen-
        dence of species, 31, 46, 57, 72,
        76
intercontinental ballistic missiles, 5
interdependence, law of, 44
interdependent life-support system,
        31–32
INTERPOL, 89
Interpol Red Notice list, 38
iron, in aquatic ecosystems, 26, 30

J
Japan
    Interpol Red Notice list, 38
    military aircraft of, 19
    oil consumption in, 15
    Southern Ocean Whale Sanctuary,
        38
job losses, 70

K
King, Martin Luther Jr., 72

L
Late Devonian event, 24–25
laws of ecology, 44
life-support system, Earth's, 25–26, 30,
        31–32
lighthouse supply vessels, 1
logging/loggers, 70, 71
loneliness, 63
Lovelock, James, 31

M
Mandela, Nelson, 21
marine biodiversity, defending, 75
marine conservation
    author sailing for, 1–2

Ordovician-Silurian extinction, 24
overpopulation, 15, 45, 71
oxygen
    in life-support system of Earth, 32
    phytoplankton manufacturing,
        30, 57
    stabilized with carbon dioxide, 24

P

Pacific Ocean, 1
Pakistan, military aircraft of, 19
pandemics, 45. *see also* COVID-19
    virus/pandemic
Passamaquoddy Bay, 1
Peacock, Doug, 55
permafrost, 11, 24, 25
Permian-Triassic extinction event, 15,
    23–24, 25, 27
pesticides, 10, 55
Phyllis Cormack (vessel), 2
phytoplankton, 26, 30, 31, 57
plant-based diet, 69, 70
plants and plant species
    in anthropocentric view, 57
    domesticated, 31, 44
    in Earth's life-support system, 26
    enslavement of, 33
    in interdependent system, 32
    in life-support system, 31
    producing oxygen, 24
plastic(s)
    ceasing production of all single-
        use, 71
    cruise ships and, 19
    removing from the ocean, 2
    tires shedding microplastics, 18
plate tectonics, 24
politicians. *see also* government
    on climate change, 11
    on job loss, 70
    sources of money for getting
        elected, 39–40
population. *See* human population
Princeton University, 40
propaganda, anti-environmentalist, 39

R

radioactive water, 35
rainforests, 58, 71
relationships (human), 63, 64
resource-based wars, 16
resource extraction, 39, 70
resources. *see also* fossil fuels
    depletion of, 15–16
    law of finite, 15, 33, 44
    reducing consumption of, 10
respiration, 26
rivers
    dammed, 31
    water in, 29, 30–31
Ross Ice Shelf, 53
Royal Canadian Mounted Police, 37
Russia
    military aircraft of, 19
    oligarchy in, 40

S

sailing, author's experiences with, 1–2
Sanders, Bernie, 39, 73
Sandoval, Jairo Mora, 36
saurian species, 25
School Strike for Climate, 74
Scleractinia (coral reefs), 17
Scott Island, 53
sea(s) and seawater
    climate change impacting, 26
    in cycle of water, 29, 30
    fish taken from, 20
    mission to stop killing of sperm
        whales in, 2–5
    moratorium on commercial fish-
        ing for, 70
    radioactive water in, 35
sea levels, 11, 24, 26
search-and-rescue vessels, 1
Sea Shepherd Conservation Society
    activities of, 75, 88
    author sailing for, 1–2
    fighting the Adani coal mine,
        Australia, 37–38
    mission of, 88–89

Watson, Paul Franklin
    accused of being an ecoterrorist,
        38
    biography, 1–2
    on dealing with reality of climate
        change, 67
    on interdependence of species, 57
    living in Antarctica, 53
    on material things, 65–66
    personal experience with a dying
        whale, 4–5, 47
    sailing experiences, 1–2
    Sea Shepherd and, 88
    on stress, 61–67
    teaching at ArtCenter College of
        Design, 58
weapons, killing whales for, 5
"wet markets," 11, 72
Wet'suwet'en Nation, 37
whales
    author's efforts to save, 2, 5
    author speaking to Haida students
        about, 49–50
    author's personal experience with
        a dying, 4–5, 47
    feces of, 30
    Japan's illegal slaughter of, 38
    killed for oil, 5
    mission to stop Soviet harpooner
        from, 2–5

reasons for sinking Icelandic
    whaling fleet, 47–48
Wilberforce, William, 72
wild animals, 33, 55–56
Wilde, Oscar, 64
wilderness
    in Antarctica, 53
    anthropocentric values and, 57–58
    big and dangerous animals in the,
        55–56
    golf courses and, 55
    importance of experiencing the,
        58–59
    people's alienation from, 54
    of the sea, 53–54, 56
    as something to subdue or destroy,
        56
    Thoreau on, 54
    threat of uncertainty and insecu-
        rity in, 56, 59
wildfires, 44. see also fires and fire-
    storms
worms, 31
Wounded Knee, South Dakota, 72–73

Y

Yucatan Peninsula, 25

Z

Zimbabwe, 58

Captain Paul Watson is a Canadian American marine-conservation activist who founded the direct-action group Sea Shepherd Conservation Society in 1977. He later became familiar to the public through Animal Planet's popular television series *Whale Wars*. Sea Shepherd's mission is to protect all ocean-dwelling marine life. Today, there are thousands of Sea Shepherd activists worldwide, working together on campaigns in more than forty countries.

Even as a boy, Watson wanted to protect animals from hunters. When he was older and had become an early member of Greenpeace, he would use daring tactics to save marine wildlife from hunters. His sailing experience was acquired through the Coast Guard and the Merchant Marine. Watson has been described as "the world's most aggressive, most determined, most active, and most effective defender of wildlife."

He is the recipient of the Genesis Award from the Humane Society of the United States and the George H.W. Bush Daily Point of Light Award. In 2002, he was inducted into the US Animal Rights Hall of Fame. In 2012, Watson became the second person, after Captain Jacques Cousteau, to receive the Medaille de l'Etoile Polaire (Polar Star Medal) Jules Verne Adventures Award, dedicated to environmentalists and adventurers. In 2019, he received a commendation from Connecticut's Governor Ned Lamont for fifty years as an environmental conservation activist.

A prolific writer, Watson has authored or coauthored more than one dozen books, including *Dealing with Climate Change and Stress, The Haunted Mariner,* and *Captain Paul Watson: Interview with a Pirate.* The documentary *Watson* is about his life.

More information can be found at seashepherd.org.

ABOUT SEA SHEPHERD

S ea Shepherd is an international nonprofit marine conservation organization founded in 1977 in Vancouver, Canada, by
Captain Paul Watson. In 1981, it incorporated in Oregon as
the Sea Shepherd Conservation Society. The organization's mission
is to protect defenseless marine wildlife and end the destruction of
habitat in our global oceans. It has earned the reputation of being
the world's most passionate and powerful protector of ocean life.

Today, Sea Shepherd has become an international movement,
with independent groups established in more than twenty countries, all working together on direct-action campaigns around the
world. These campaigns have safeguarded whales, dolphins, seals,
sharks, penguins, turtles, fish, krill, and aquatic birds from poach-
ing, unsustainable fishing, habitat destruction, and exploitive
captivity. Although much of the action takes place on the open sea,
Sea Shepherd remains a grassroots movement that engages thousands of volunteers who participate in land-based actions to clean
up marine debris on beaches, protect coastal nesting habitats, and
educate the public about its mission.

From its earliest years, Sea Shepherd has embraced the man-
date of the United Nations World Charter for Nature to uphold
international conservation laws. Its fleet of twelve vessels makes
up the largest private navy on the planet. Sea Shepherd collabo-
rates with governments, allowing them to share its ships in order
to intervene and enforce the law.

The mission of Sea Shepherd's legal team is to save marine
wildlife and preserve habitats by enforcing, strengthening, and
developing protective laws, treaties, policies, and practices world-

wide. It works collaboratively with governments to stop illegal, unreported, and unregulated fishing in sovereign waters; encourages public engagement; and litigates against irresponsible actions, which includes working with law-enforcement agencies, such as INTERPOL, to help bring poachers to justice.

"Our commitment has led us to protect marine wildlife—including endangered or threatened species—and their delicate habitats. We have cut illegal nets, cleaned vital ecosystems, shut down illegal operations in contentious waters, and even delivered humanitarian supplies. We never stop, because the survival of our ocean is a constant challenge. It is an enduring commitment and a long-term solution.

Life began in the ocean. We must defend, conserve, and protect it. Now and always."

—SEA SHEPHERD
CONSERVATION SOCIETY

GROUNDSWELL BOOKS
SOLUTIONS FOR A SUSTAINABLE WORLD

For more books that inspire readers to create a healthy,
sustainable planet for future generations, visit
BookPubCo.com.

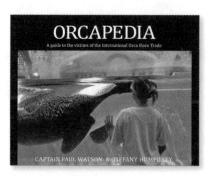

Orcapedia:
A Guide to the Victims of the
International Orca Slave Trade
Captain Paul Watson and Tiffany Humphrey
978-1-57067-398-6 • $24.95

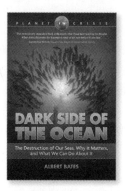

Dark Side of the Ocean:
The Destruction of Our Seas, Why It Matters,
and What We Can Do About It
Albert Bates
978-1-57067-394-8 • $12.95

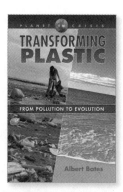

Transforming Plastic:
From Pollution to Evolution
Albert Bates
978-1-57067-371-9 • $9.95

Cooking' Up a Storm:
Sea Stories and Vegan Recipes
Laura Dakin
978-1-57067-312-2 • $24.95

Purchase these titles from your favorite book source or buy them directly from
Book Publishing Company • PO Box 99 • Summertown, TN 38483 • 1-888-260-8458
Free shipping and handling on all orders